CW00607136

Beautiful & Calming

ORIGAMI

h

hinkler

hinkler

Published by Hinkler Books Pty Ltd 2016
45–55 Fairchild Street
Heatherton Victoria 3202 Australia
www.hinkler.com.au

Design, layout, cover & photography © Hinkler Books Pty Ltd 2008, 2014, 2016
Text, models & folding techniques © Matthew Gardiner and contributing artists 2008
Paper designs © Shutterstock.com or Hinkler Books Pty Ltd
Images © Hinkler Books Pty Ltd or Shutterstock.com

Author: Matthew Gardiner
Cover design: Sam Grimmer
Cover photography: Ned Meldrum
Internal design: Trudi Webb and Hinkler Design Studio

ISBN: 978 1 4889 3209 0

Printed and bound in China

CONTENTS

ABOUT ORIGAMI

What is origami?

Origami is a curious sounding word because it is not English, but Japanese in origin. Ori, from the root verb oru, means 'to fold' and kami is one of the many terms for paper. In the purest renditions, origami creates an intended shape from a single sheet of paper with no cutting, gluing, taping or any other fastening device allowed. To create less rigid versions one may make small cuts as in kirigami ('cut paper'), or long slits as in senbazuru – where a single sheet is effectively divided into a number of smaller, still connected squares.

The origin of origami

No-one really knows when origami was invented. We do know that paper had to be invented first, so we can safely say that it is less than 2000 years old, but an exact date, even to the nearest century, cannot be authentically established. Despite its Japanese name, some claim that it is Chinese in origin; this cannot be entirely discounted since many art forms now claimed by others can be traced back to mainland China.

One reason for origami's hazy history is that for many centuries there was almost no documentation on how to do it. The oldest book known to contain origami-like instructions, the *Kanamodo*, is from the 17th century, yet older woodblock prints show paper folding. The oldest example of a book written about practising origami for entertainment is *Hiden Senbazuru Orikata* from 1797. The title roughly translated means 'the secret technique of folding one thousand cranes'.

There are around one hundred designs known as 'traditional origami', which were passed from hand to hand in Japanese culture: typically a mother showing a child, or children sharing the knowledge among themselves. In fact, until the middle of the 20th century, origami was thought of as something that women did as decorations for weddings, funerals and other ceremonial occasions, or something that young children did as a recreational pursuit.

After the Second World War people from around the world started to visit Japan in greater numbers, and Japanese citizens increased their travel to other countries. Through this exposure, origami started to spread throughout the world, especially through exchange students – those young ambassadors of Japanese culture. The form began to spread across genders and cultures. Today, a finished model can be made and displayed for your own pleasure, or given as a gift, cementing a friendship through paper folding.

How to Fold

BY: Matthew Gardiner

The key to high-quality origami is the quality of each fold. There are many kinds of folds, but the principles described below can be applied to most folds. Origami paper has a coloured (or patterned) side and a white side. When diagrams refer to the coloured side, it is to indicate which side will be dominant in the final model.

1

Gently lift the bottom corner to the top corner. Don't crease yet, just hold the paper in position.

2

Line up the corners exactly. The image above is not aligned correctly.

3

The corners are exactly aligned; there is no visible difference.

4

Hold the corner with one hand, and slide the forefinger of the other hand down to the bottom.

5

Crease from the centre to the edge. Check that the crease goes exactly through the corner.

6

Crease from the centre to the edge on the other side to complete the fold.

In these two introductory folds, the edges and corners are the references. Use existing creases, corners, edges, intersections of creases, and points to make sure your fold is accurate.

1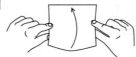

Lift the bottom edge to the top edge.

2

Align the corners and then align the edges on one side.

3

Align the opposite corner and edges so that both sides are perfectly aligned.

4

Hold one corner and crease from the centre to the edge.

5

Crease from the centre to the other edge so all corners and edges are aligned.

Symbols

BY: Matthew Gardiner

Lines

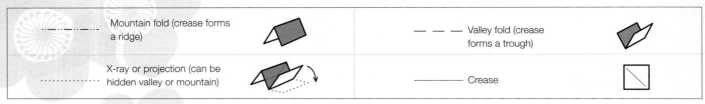

Mountain fold (crease forms a ridge)

Valley fold (crease forms a trough)

X-ray or projection (can be hidden valley or mountain)

Crease

Arrows

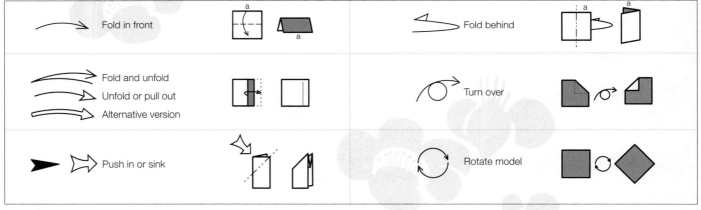

Fold in front

Fold behind

Fold and unfold
Unfold or pull out
Alternative version

Turn over

Push in or sink

Rotate model

Extras

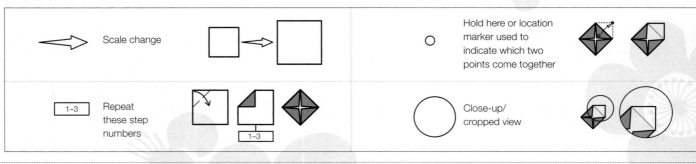

Scale change

Hold here or location marker used to indicate which two points come together

1–3   Repeat these step numbers

Close-up/ cropped view

TYPES OF FOLDS

BY: MATTHEW GARDINER

BOOK FOLD

Valley fold one edge to another, like closing a book.

CUPBOARD FOLD

Fold both edges to the middle crease, like closing two cupboard doors.

BLINTZ FOLD

Fold all corners to the middle. This was named after a style of pastry called a blintz.

INSIDE REVERSE FOLD

The spine of the existing fold is reversed and pushed inside.

OUTSIDE REVERSE FOLD

The spine of the existing fold is reversed and wrapped outside.

PETAL FOLD   The petal fold is found in the crane base.

1	2	3	4	5
Fold top layer to the centre crease.	Fold and unfold the top triangle down. Unfold flaps.	Lift the top layer upwards.	Step 3 in progress; the model is 3D. Fold the top layer inwards on existing creases.	Completed petal fold.

SQUASH FOLD   A squash fold is the symmetrical flattening of a point. The flattening movement is known as squashing the point.

1	2	3	4
Pre-crease on the line for the squash fold.	Open up the paper by inserting your finger. Fold the paper across.	As you put the paper in place, gently squash the point into a symmetrical shape.	Completed squash fold.

IRIS

MODEL: TRADITIONAL, JAPAN
DIAGRAM: MATTHEW GARDINER

The iris takes its name from the Greek word for rainbow. Its name reflects the wide range of colours that appear in different species of iris. This model looks best when folded from blended or two-toned paper.

The iris is a popular symbol, appearing on the flag of Brussels, and in the fleur-de-lis, the symbol of Florence, Italy.

1

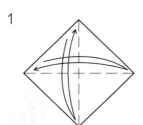

Fold and unfold diagonals.
Turn over.

2

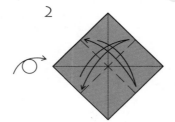

Book fold and unfold.

3

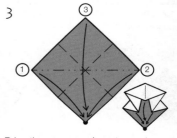

Bring three corners down to meet bottom corner. Start with corners 1 and 2 together followed by corner 3.

4

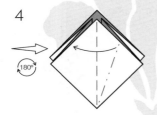

Rotate the model 180°.
Pre-crease then squash fold.

5

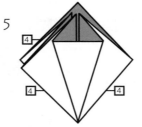

Repeat step 4 on the other three sides.

6

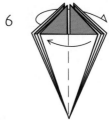

Turn top and back layers over.

7

Fold top layer edges to meet the middle.

8

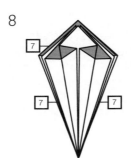

Repeat step 7 to both sides and behind.

9

Fold front petal down.

10

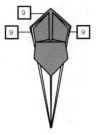

Repeat step 9 on all three sides making the model 3D. Start with both side petals followed by the back petal.

11

Completed iris.

Six Point Star

MODEL: Darren Scott
DIAGRAM: Darren Scott

This model locks very strongly together although it's a little tricky to assemble. However once you have it assembled, it will not come apart easily. It uses a paper lock, which is a sequence of folds that when completed is hard to open. You will need six pieces of origami paper for this model.

This is a great decoration, particularly as its stable construction makes it durable.

1

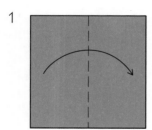

Start with the square coloured side up. Book fold.

2

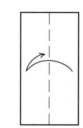

Fold the front layer in half and unfold.

3

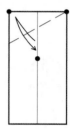

Fold the top left corner so it lies along the crease made in step 2 and unfold.

4

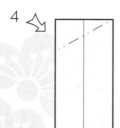

Sink the top left corner along the crease made in step 3.

5

Fold the top right corner down so it lies along the left edge.

6

Fold the top layer to the left and unfold. This will be used to lock the units in place later.

7

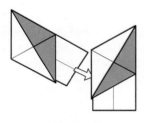

Repeat steps 1-6 until you have a total of 6 units. Insert two units together.

8

Fold to the left and tuck under flap. This locks the units together.

9

Unfold the lock. These will be refolded in steps 13 and 14.

10

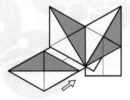

Add the third unit.

11

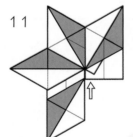

Add the remaining units.

12

Add the remaining units.

This will be the result. Now we need to lock the units in place.

13

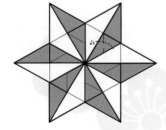

Refold the crease from step 9 to lock the units together.

14

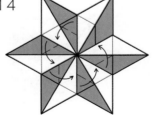

Lock the remaining units in place.

15

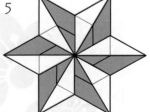

Completed six point star.

MASU BOX

MODEL: TRADITIONAL, JAPAN
DIAGRAM: MATTHEW GARDINER

The masu box is a very practical origami model. Traditionally it was used as a measure for rice, as certain sheet sizes produced a set volume of rice. The masu has many new variations, and perhaps the best variation is that by making a slightly bigger or smaller box, you can make a lid or a base.

The masu box is handy for holding almost anything.

1

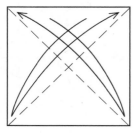

Begin white side up. Fold and unfold diagonals.

2

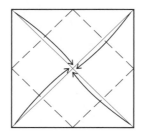

Blintz fold.

3

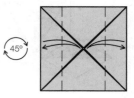

Cupboard fold and unfold.

4

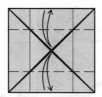

Cupboard fold and unfold the other edges.

5

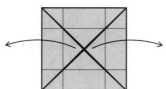

Unfold two side points.

6

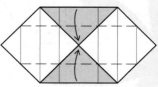

Fold on existing creases.

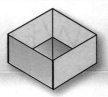

7

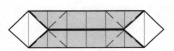

Fold and unfold on diagonals.

8

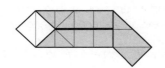

Step 7 in progress.

9

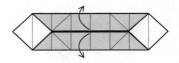

Lift sides to 90°.

10

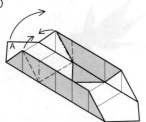

To make the side of the box, lift point A upwards – the existing sides will naturally collapse to points.

11

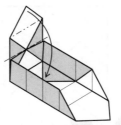

Fold the point down into the box, and press the point to the centre.

12

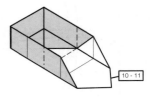

Repeat steps 10-11 on this side.

13

Completed masu box.

WENTWORTH DISH

MODEL: NICK ROBINSON
DIAGRAM: NICK ROBINSON

Nick Robinson has a penchant for creating simple paper dishes that have elegant forms and equally elegant paper locks. The finished shape of this Wentworth dish has variations that can be achieved by altering the angle of one fold.

The dishes Nick Robinson is so fond of folding are inspired by the work of origami artist Philip Shen.

1

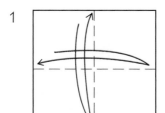

Fold and unfold.

2

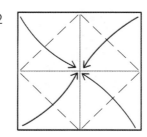

Blintz fold. Turn over.
Rotate the paper 45°.

3

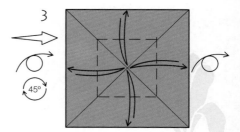

Fold and unfold edges to the centre as shown. Turn over.

4

Fold corners inside.
Turn over again.

5

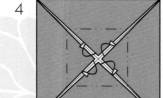

Fold and unfold.

6

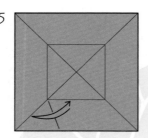

Fold the top layer to the left and unfold.

7

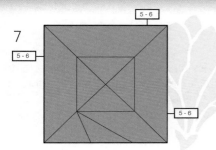

Repeat steps 5-6 on other three sides.

8

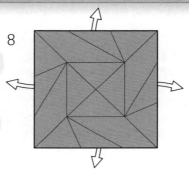

Unfold the sheet completely.

9

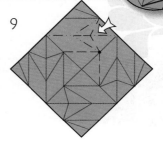

Sink fold. Make sure that the black dot goes down.

10

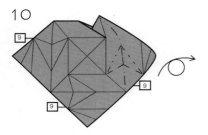

Repeat step 9 on the other three sides. Turn over.

11

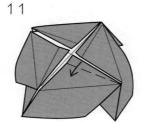

To lock the bottom fold up.

12

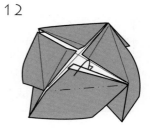

Tuck flap inside for a white centre.

13

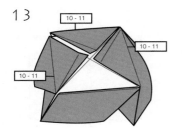

Repeat steps 10-11 on other three sides.

14

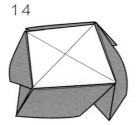

Completed back. Turn over.

15

Completed dish.

WALKING CRAB

MODEL: SHOKO AOYAGI
DIAGRAM: SHOKO AOYAGI

The walking crab is a fun design that walks sideways when you tap it. Shoko Aoyagi is well known for her fun origami style – she likes to use stick-on eyes to add character to her origami creations. Cut out circles of white and black paper and glue them together, or use pre-cut circles that are available at office-supply stores.

The walking crab is a contemporary Japanese design.

1

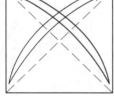

Fold and unfold diagonals, then turn over.

2

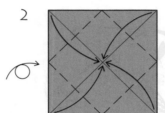

Blintz fold.

3

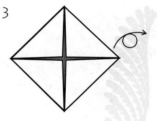

Completed step 2. Turn over.

4

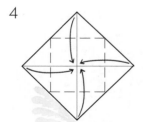

Blintz fold again.

5

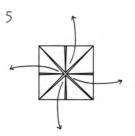

Completely unfold the paper.

6

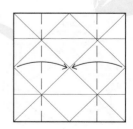

Then fold sides to centre in a cupboard fold.

7

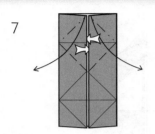

Bring both corners forwards
and squash fold.

8

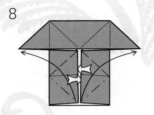

Repeat step 7 on other end.

9

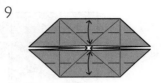

Fold and unfold top and bottom
edge to the centre.

10

Open up pockets.

11

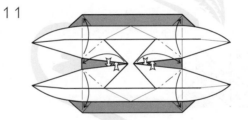

This shows the pockets open. Lift up inside
corners, and fold the edges outwards.

12

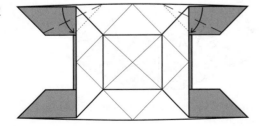

Fold edge to corner.

13

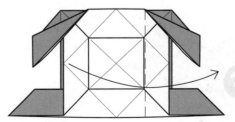

Fold over.

14

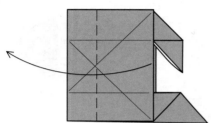

Fold over.

15

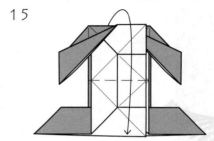

Fold in half through all layers.

16

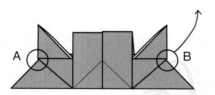

Hold point A with one hand. Pull point B upwards.

17

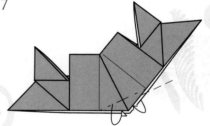

Fold inside the base of the front flap as shown.
Repeat on the other side. Rotate the model 25°.

18

Completed walking crab.

19

When you tap point C, the crab will walk sideways.
Attach eyes.

SAMURAI HELMET

MODEL: TRADITIONAL, JAPAN
DIAGRAM: MATTHEW GARDINER

The samurai helmet, or kabuto, can be made from a large square of paper and be worn as a paper warrior's hat.

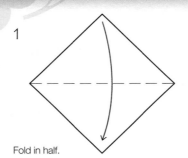

1

Fold in half.

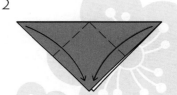

2

Fold corners down.

3

Fold flaps up.

4

Fold top corners outwards.

5

Fold the top layer only.

6

Fold up.

7

Fold up, then tuck inside the helmet.

8

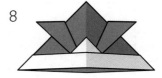

The finished samurai helmet.

LUNCH BAG

MODEL: DARREN SCOTT
DIAGRAM: DARREN SCOTT

The no-glue lunch bag will come in handy for storing all sorts of things, not just your lunch. Try varying the width and height of the paper you start with to suit the object you want to store.

This design means you can make something both pretty and practical!

1

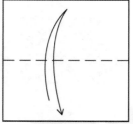

Start with a square white side up. Book fold and unfold.

2

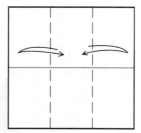

Divide the square into thirds vertically, and unfold.

3

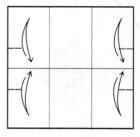

Divide the square into thirds horizontally. This time just make small pinch marks at the edges.

4

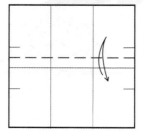

Make a fold between the top pinch mark and the centre crease. Unfold.

5

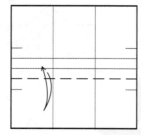

Repeat step 4 using the bottom pinch marks.

6

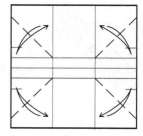

Create the diagonal creases and unfold.

7

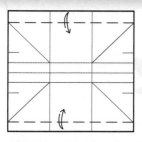

Using the diagonal creases as landmarks, fold the top and bottom edges. Unfold.

8

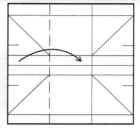

Fold a third to the right using the crease made in step 3.

9

Using the existing creases start forming the side of the bag.

10

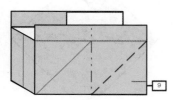

This should be the result. Repeat step 9 on the right-hand side.

11

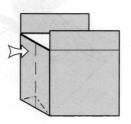

Push the side edge inwards and bring the top edges together.

12

Fold the corners down to meet the creases made in step 7.

13

Refold the creases made in step 7.

14

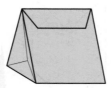

Completed lunch bag.

PAJARITO

MODEL: TRADITIONAL, SPAIN
DIAGRAM: MATTHEW GARDINER

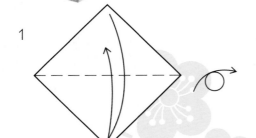

Pajarito, or 'Little Bird', is the most famous traditional design from Spain. Historically, Spanish origami was born from the geometric fascination of the Moors. The model requires a 3D transformation move at the end. Be careful when folding to make sure the mountain and valley folds are placed correctly. Then the final move will be almost 'natural' for the paper.

The pajarito is the icon of Spanish origami. 'Papiroflexia' is the Spanish way of saying paper folding.

1

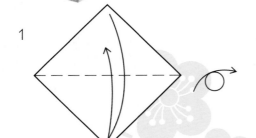

Begin white side up.
Fold and unfold diagonal. Turn over.

2

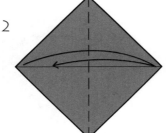

Fold and unfold diagonal.

3

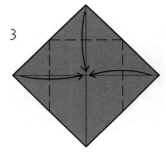

Fold three corners to the centre.

4

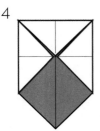

Completed step 3.
Turn over.

5

Fold top corners down to centre point.

6

Fold and unfold, be careful to only crease as shown.

7

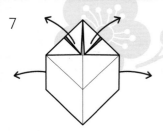

Unfold corners and side flaps.
Turn over.

8

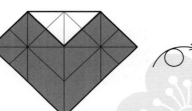

Your model should look like this.
Turn over.

9

Fold on existing creases. Pay attention to the
mountain and valley folds.

10

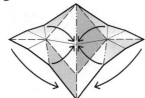

The 3D move in progress.

11

Completed pajarito.

SPANISH BOX

MODEL: TRADITIONAL, SPAIN
DIAGRAM: MATTHEW GARDINER

The traditional Spanish box was brought to the world origami stage by the British magician and origami expert Robert Harbin during his famous BBC television series. It's a practical decorative model, and if you use a 30cm (12in) sheet, or larger, of stiff card you can create a strong vessel for sweets and foods at parties.

The Spanish box is so named because of the decorative pleating on the rim of the box.

1

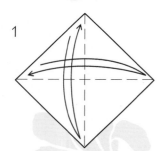

Fold and unfold diagonals.

2

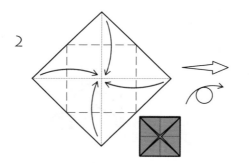

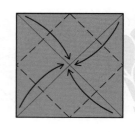

Blintz fold.
Turn over.

3

Blintz fold again.

4

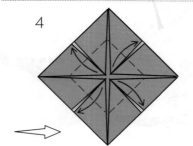

Fold top layers from the centre to corners.

5

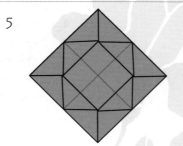

Completed step 4. Turn over.

6

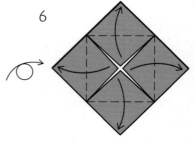

Fold top layers from the centre to corners.

7

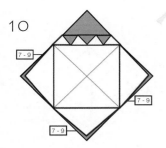

Detail of corner.

8

Fold over as shown.

9

Completed step 8.

10

7 - 9
7 - 9
7 - 9

Repeat steps 7-9 on the three remaining corners.

11

Pinch each corner as shown by the white arrows making the box 3D.

12

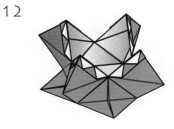

Completed Spanish box.

TATO

MODEL: TRADITIONAL, JAPAN
DIAGRAM: MATTHEW GARDINER

The tato is a form of paper purse or puzzle in Japan. Tatogami is folded paper that is used to store expensive kimonos, however this tato design is for smaller objects. Origami masters Shuzo Fujimoto and Michio Uchiyama are renowned for their innovation in expanding tato designs. The primary method involves dividing the square radially, in this case into eight segments, that fold inward over each other.

Tato can be folded from fabric or two laminated sheets of paper for maximum durability and effect.

1

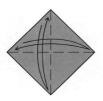

Start coloured side up. Fold and unfold diagonals. Turn over.

2

Book fold and unfold.

3

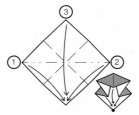

Collapse into the preliminary base.

4

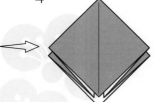

The preliminary base.

5

Fold edges of top layer to the centre.

6

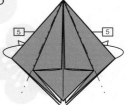

Repeat step 5 on the other side.

7

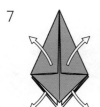

Unfold to a flat sheet.

8

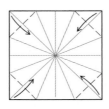

Fold corners in at the intersection of existing creases. This makes a perfect octagon.

9

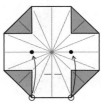

Fold the edge to the middle. Be careful to only crease as shown.

10

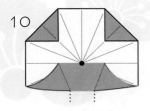

Step 9 in progress. Only crease between the dotted lines.

11

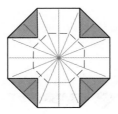

Repeat step 9 all around the octagon.

12

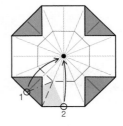

Fold point 1 to the middle. Then fold point 2. This will create a point with the greyed-out paper. Fold this point to the left. Look ahead to step 13 to see the result.

13

Fold the point marked by the circle to the point marked by the dot.

14

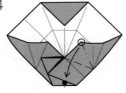

Repeat step 13 on the remaining points. The last point needs to be tucked under the first point.

15

The finished tato. To open the purse gently pull on two opposite points.

SWAN

MODEL: TRADITIONAL, JAPAN
DIAGRAM: MATTHEW GARDINER

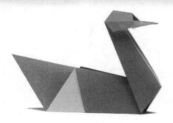

This simple origami model reflects the elegant form of a swan gliding across the waters of a lake.

1

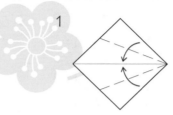

Pre-crease diagonal. Fold sides to the middle.

2

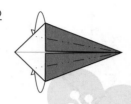

Mountain fold both sides to the middle.

3

Fold in half.

4

Outside reverse fold the neck.

5

Outside reverse fold the head.

6

Pull out hidden paper on both sides of the head.

7

Pleat then double reverse fold the head to form the beak.

8

Completed swan.

WATER LILY

MODEL: TRADITIONAL, JAPAN
DIAGRAM: MATTHEW GARDINER

The water lily is a beautiful form, invoking the charm of the lily floating on the water.

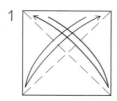

1

Fold and unfold diagonals.

2

Fold corners to the centre.

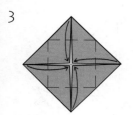

3

Fold corners to the centre again.

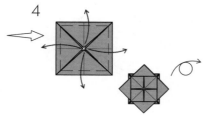

4

Fold indicated corners outwards leaving a small gap at the edges. Turn over.

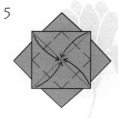

5

While folding the indicated corners to the centre, the model will change into 3D.

6

Completed step 5. Turn over.

7

Fold indicated corners outside leaving a little gap at the edges. Turn over.

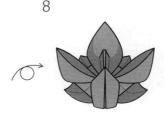

8

Completed water lily.

PAPER CRANE

MODEL: TRADITIONAL, JAPAN
DIAGRAM: MATTHEW GARDINER

The traditional Japanese paper crane or *orizuru* is famous throughout the world. It is a symbol of origami and a symbol of peace. An ancient Japanese legend says that whoever folds 1000 cranes will be granted a wish.

Today, in Hiroshima, stands the peace memorial of Sadako Sasaki built by her classmates in her memory to inspire peace around the world. Sadako was a victim of 'atomic-bomb disease' and she folded cranes until she died. She never gave up on her wish to be well.

1

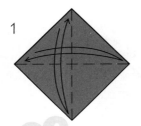

Start coloured side up.
Fold and unfold diagonals.
Turn over.

2

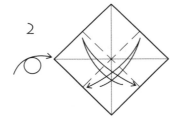

Book fold and unfold.

3

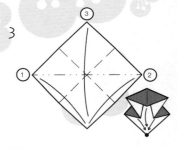

Bring three corners down to meet bottom corner. Start with corners 1 and 2 together followed by corner 3.

4

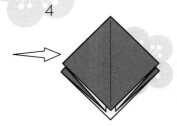

Completed preliminary base.

5

Fold top layer to the centre crease.

6

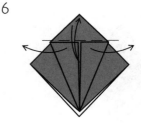

Fold and unfold the top triangle down. Unfold flaps.

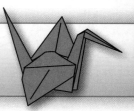

7

Lift the top layer upwards.

8

Step 7 in progress; the model is 3D. Fold the top layer inwards on existing creases.

9

Step 7 completed; the model will be flat. Turn over.

10

5 - 9

Repeat steps 5-9 on this side.

11

Narrow the bottom points on the top layer only. Repeat behind.

12

Reverse fold the bottom point upwards.

13

Your model should look like this. Repeat on the other side.

14

Completed body. The next steps focus on the head.

15

Reverse fold the point to create the head.

MODEL: TRADITIONAL, JAPAN
DIAGRAM: MATTHEW GARDINER

16

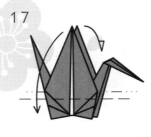

Head completed.

17

Fold wings down.

18

Pull the wings gently to shape the body.

19

Completed paper crane – repeat 1000 times for a wish.

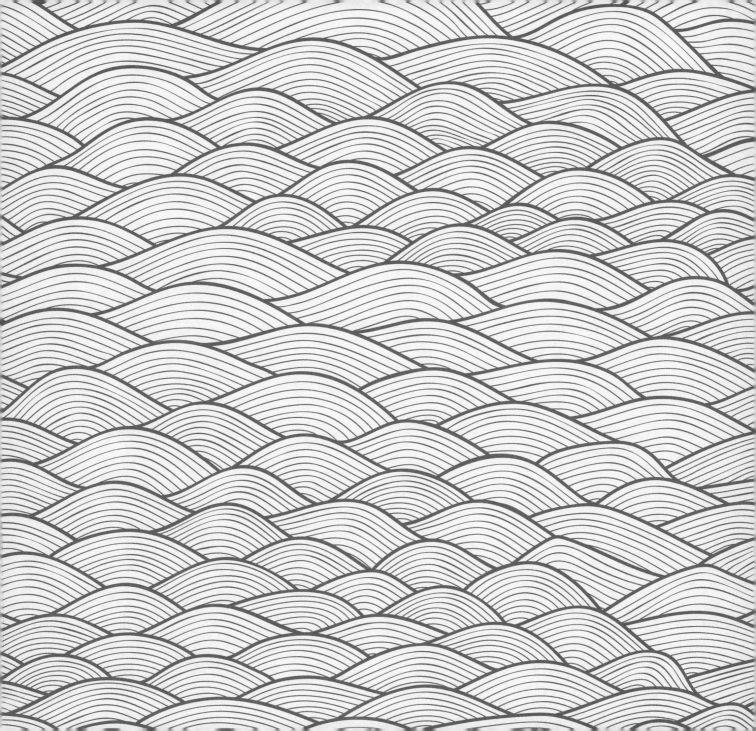

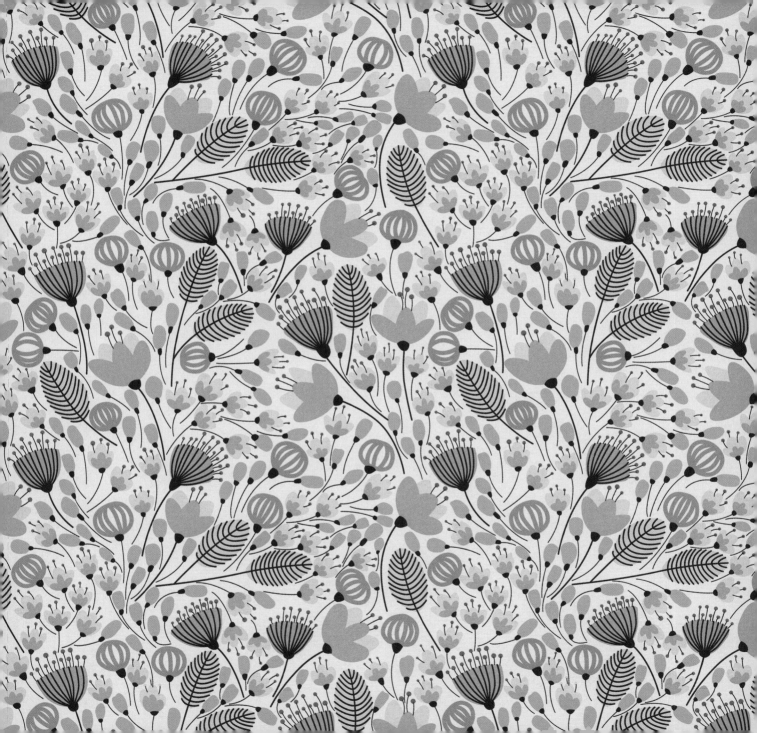

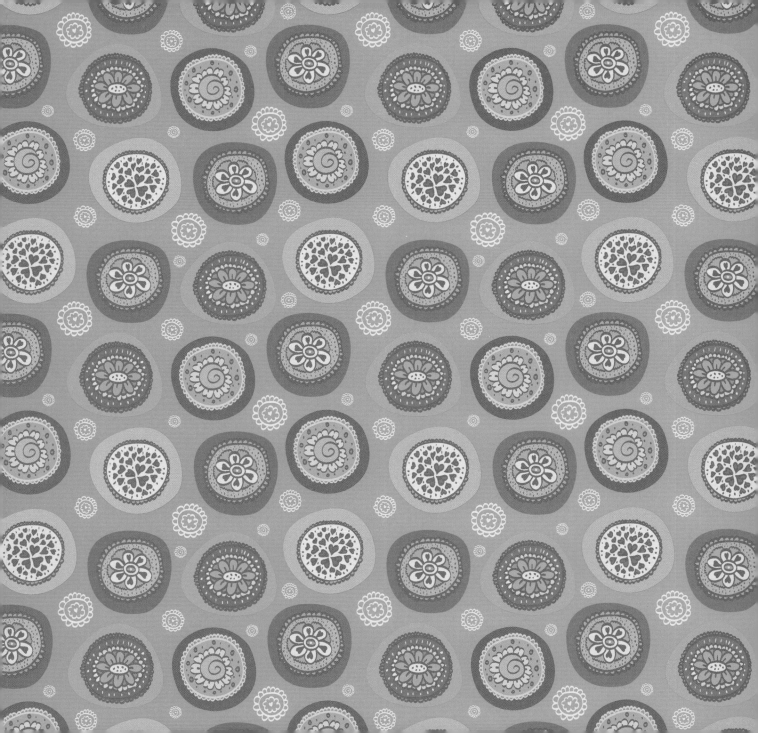

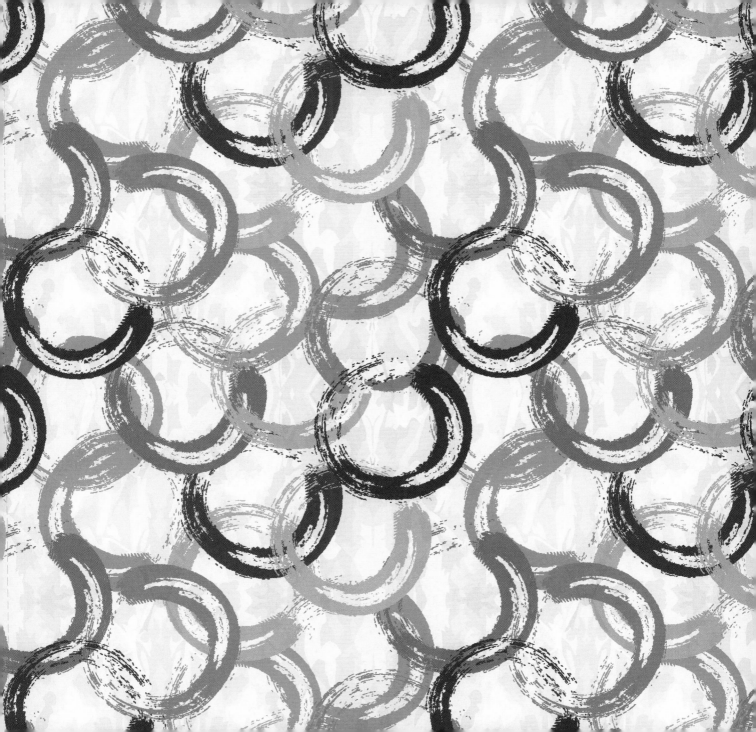

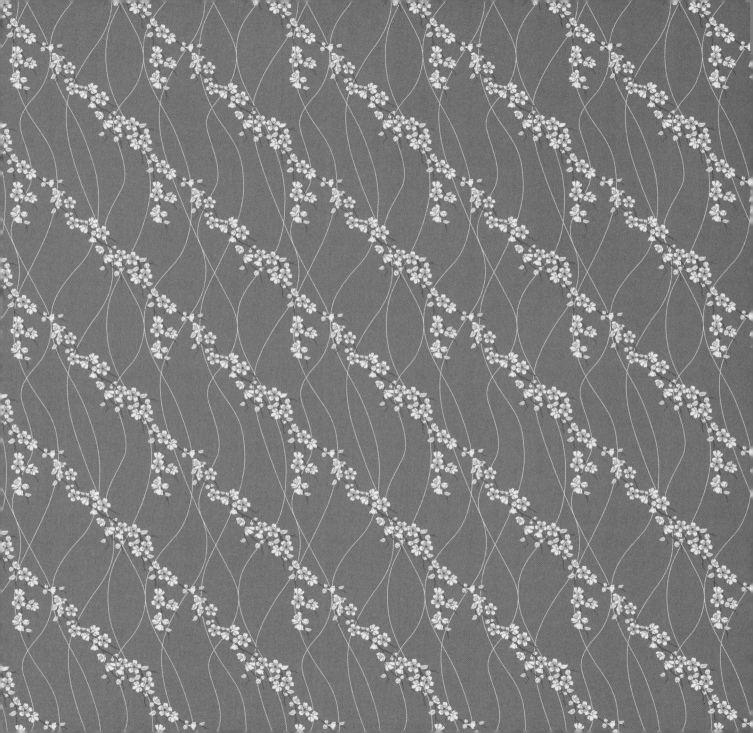

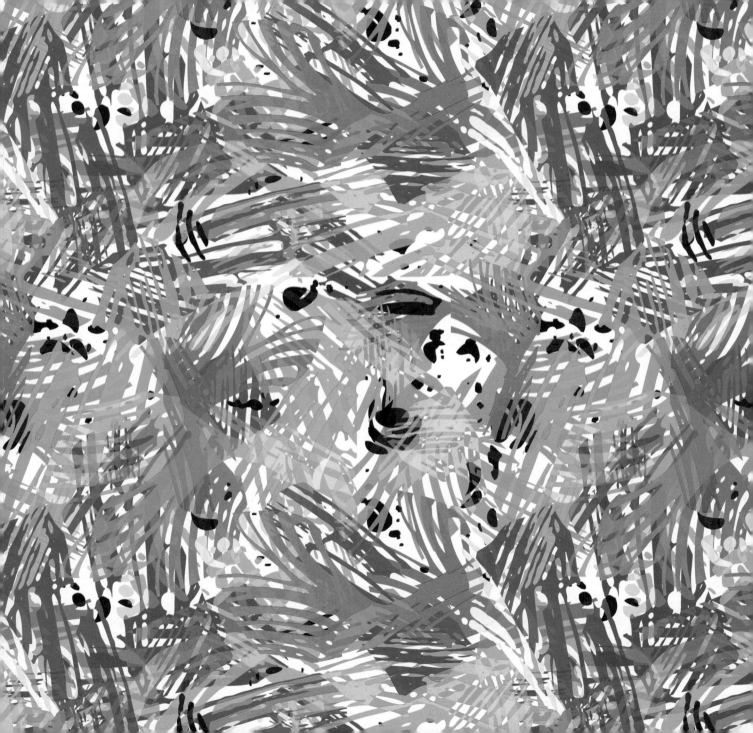

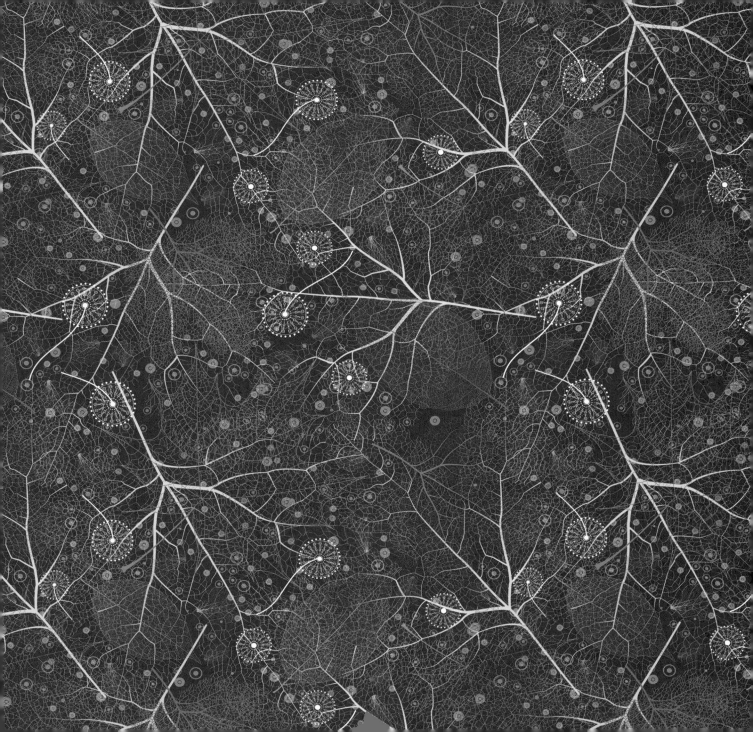

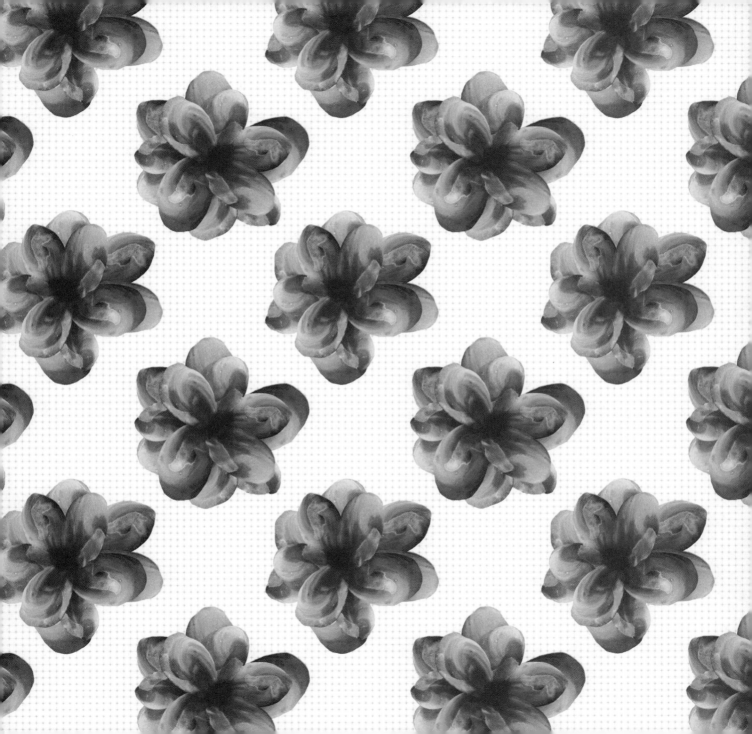